The symbols represent the twelve sons (Genesis 49).

Dan

Gad

Asher

Naphtali

Joseph

Benjamin

FROM THE AUTHOR

◆

I chose most of these stories because the characters in them have been favourites of mine since my own childhood: Zacchaeus, the pompous little man who yet climbed a tree; Bartimaeus, who would *not* be silent when he had something desperately important he wanted to say; Peter – impetuous, vulnerable, lovable – and all the others. All real people, in the limelight for just a moment; yet their stories are vividly alive even today.

Marjorie Newman

Designed by Bob Swan
Typeset in Novarese by Face
Printed in Belgium

ISBN 0-8317-0830-1

SMITHMARK books are available for bulk purchase for sales promotion and premium use.
For details write or telephone the Manager of Special Sales, SMITHMARK Publishers Inc.,
112 Madison Avenue, New York, NY 10016. (212) 532-6600

SMITHMARK

BIBLE PEOPLE
Stories retold by Marjorie Newman
Illustrations by Lorraine Calaora

CONTENTS

OLD TESTAMENT

6   NOAH
     Genesis 6: 5-22; 7:8; 9: 8-17

7   LOT'S WIFE
     Genesis 18: 32,33; 19: 1-29

7   ABRAHAM AND ISAAC
     Genesis 22: 1-18

8   ESAU AND JACOB
     Genesis 27: 1-45; 28: 1-5

9   JOSEPH
     Genesis 37: 2-35

10   BABY MOSES
     Exodus 1: 7-22; 2: 1-10

11   JOSHUA
     Joshua 6

12   SAMSON AND DELILAH
     Judges 16: 4-30

13   RUTH AND NAOMI
     Ruth 1: 1-19

13   SAMUEL
     1 Samuel 1: 1-28; 2: 18-21; 3

14   DAVID AND GOLIATH
     1 Samuel 17: 1-51

15   THE QUEEN OF SHEBA
     1 Kings 10: 1-13

15   ELIJAH
     1 Kings 17: 1-6

16   NAAMAN VISITS ELISHA
     2 Kings 5: 1-9

16   ESTHER
     Esther 1; 2

17   ISAIAH
     excerpts from the book of Isaiah

18   DANIEL
     Daniel 6

19   JONAH
     Book of Jonah

NEW TESTAMENT

20   ELIZABETH AND ZACHARIAS
     Luke 1: 5-25; 57-66

21   SIMEON AND ANNA
     Luke 2: 21-38

22   JESUS' DISCIPLES
     Luke 10: 2

22   JAIRUS' DAUGHTER
     Luke 8: 40-42; 49-56

23   THE BOY WITH THE LOAVES AND FISHES
     Matthew 14: 13-21; Mark 6: 30-45;
     Luke 9: 11-17; John 6: 5-13

23   THE TEN LEPERS
     Luke 17: 11-19

24   BARTIMAEUS
     Mark 10: 50; Luke 18: 35-43

25   ZACCHAEUS
     Luke 19

26   MARY, MARTHA AND LAZARUS
     Luke 10: 38-42; John 11: 1-54

26   THE WIDOW IN THE TEMPLE
     Mark 12: 41-43; Luke 21: 1-4

27   PETER
     John 21: 1-19

28   THE LAME MAN
     Acts 3: 1-10

28   PHILIP AND THE ETHIOPIAN
     Acts 8: 26-38

29   PAUL
     Acts 9: 1-31

30   INDEX

THE OLD TESTAMENT

NOAH

God looked at the world He had made, and He was sad. The people had grown very wicked. Only one man – Noah – still loved Him.

So God said to Noah, "I shall send a great flood. All the life on earth will be destroyed. But don't be afraid! You and I will make a covenant – an agreement. If you obey Me, you and your family will be saved."

Then God told Noah to build an Ark, giving him the exact measurements. Noah listened, puzzled. Why must the Ark be so big, just for himself, his wife, his three sons and their wives?

God explained. "You must take into the Ark with you one pair of every living creature. Seven pairs of some of them. You must also take enough food."

Noah set to work. His neighbours laughed. But Noah kept on working.

When everything was prepared, the living creatures *came* to Noah. Amazed, Noah and his family led them into the Ark. And God shut the door.

After seven days it began to rain. For forty days and forty nights it rained. The whole earth was covered. But the Ark floated safely.

The rain stopped. The earth dried, clean and fresh. Out of the Ark came Noah, his family and all the creatures. And God put a rainbow in the sky, the sign of His covenant that never again would He destroy all His creation with a flood.

LOT'S WIFE

The people of Sodom were very wicked; so God decided to destroy the city with sulphur and fire. Only Lot's family were to be saved. Angel messengers told them to run, and not look back. Lot and his daughters obeyed; but Lot's wife *did* look back; and she was turned into a pillar of salt.

ABRAHAM AND ISAAC

Abraham had one son, Isaac, whom he loved very much. God began to be afraid that Abraham would put his love for his son even above obedience to God. So He spoke to Abraham. "Take Isaac to the mountains, and sacrifice him there."

Abraham could hardly believe what he was hearing. But he had always loved and obeyed God...

Sadly he set out, calling Isaac to come with him. When they were nearly there Isaac said suddenly, "Father – I have the wood, and you have the knife. But where is the lamb we will sacrifice?"

Somehow Abraham managed to answer. "God will provide the lamb."

At the exact place that God had shown him Abraham built an altar. He arranged the wood on it. Then, with tears in his eyes, he tied Isaac with a rope and laid *him* on the altar. He raised the knife...

But an angel of the Lord cried, "Stop! Don't harm the boy! By being ready to obey you have already shown that you love and trust God above everything else."

Joyfully, Abraham freed Isaac. Seeing a ram caught in the thorns nearby, Abraham took it and offered it to God as a thanksgiving sacrifice.

Then, together, Abraham and Isaac returned home.

ESAU AND JACOB

Esau and Jacob were twins; but Esau had been born first. So *he* should have been given a special blessing, and all his father Isaac's possessions as soon as Isaac died. Jacob tricked Esau, and Isaac. He got the blessing and the promise of the inheritance for himself. But then Jacob began to be afraid of Esau's anger...

He decided to go into hiding, to his Uncle Laban. All alone, Jacob hurried over the hills. But night was coming. He would have to rest.

Choosing a stone to use as a pillow, Jacob lay down. He pulled his cloak around him, and tried to sleep.

And he had a dream. He saw a ladder reaching from the ground beside him up to Heaven. Angels went up and down; and God himself stood at the top.

God spoke to Jacob. He promised that Jacob's family should be specially blessed, that God would be with him wherever he went, and that He would one day bring him safely back to this land.

Jacob awoke. "Surely this is the gate of Heaven, and I didn't know!" he trembled.

At daybreak he took the pillow-stone, stood it up on end, and poured oil over it. "I name this place 'Bethel'," he said. "And I make a promise. If God guards me and keeps me, He shall be my God. And of all that He gives me, I will give a tenth back to Him."

Then Jacob journeyed on.

JOSEPH

◆

Joseph was his father Jacob's favourite; and his ten older half-brothers were jealous. Joseph had dreams which he said meant that his family *bowed down* to him. His brothers began to hate him.

One day Jacob said to Joseph, "Your brothers have been away a long time with the sheep. Go and see if they're all right."

Cheerfully Joseph set out, wearing the coat of many colours which his father had made for him. His brothers saw him coming. "Now's our chance to be rid of him!" they snarled.

They threw him into a pit, meaning to leave him to starve. Only his brother Reuben was sorry, and planned to rescue Joseph later. But while Reuben was away checking the sheep, a camel-train came by. Traders, on their way to Egypt! The other brothers said, "Let's sell Joseph! We shall still be rid of him – but we shall have some money as well!"

So Joseph was sold to be a slave.

When Reuben came back and discovered what had happened he was very upset; but it was too late.

The brothers dipped Joseph's torn coat into the blood of one of their sheep. They took the coat to Jacob, saying they had found it on the path. Jacob cried out, "My son has been killed by wild animals!" He wept, and no one could comfort him.

But God was with Joseph, and many surprising things were to happen before he died.

9

BABY MOSES

Pharaoh had ordered that all baby boys must be killed – and Miriam had a new baby brother! He needed a safe hiding place.

Miriam watched as her mother Jochabed dried some rushes from the nearby river and wove a basket-cradle from them. Jochabed covered the outside with pitch to make it waterproof; and Miriam began to guess her mother's plan.

They tucked the sleeping baby into the basket. Jochabed picked it up. She and Miriam crept down to the river bank, and Jochabed hid the baby in the bulrushes.

"Hide nearby, and keep watch!" Jochabed told Miriam. Then she went home, so that no one would wonder where she was.

It was very quiet, until – Miriam heard voices! She peeped out. The princess, daughter of the Pharaoh, was coming with her maids to bathe! Miriam watched helplessly as one of the maids found the basket, and took it to the princess.
The princess opened the lid – and saw the baby. Miriam couldn't bear to watch...

But she heard the princess say, "It's one of the Israelite babies! I should like to keep him!"

Then Miriam ran to the princess. "Shall I fetch a nurse to look after him?" she cried.

"Yes please!" smiled the princess.

Miriam ran and fetched her mother! And the princess paid Jochabed to take care of the baby!

When he was old enough he went to live at the palace. The princess named him Moses, and he grew up to have many special adventures.

JOSHUA

Joshua was leading the people of Israel. He knew that if the Israelites were to enter the land God had promised to them they would first have to capture the city of Jericho. But how? All Jericho's gates were tightly locked, and its walls were very thick.

Then God spoke, telling him what to do. Joshua listened in amazement! This would be a strange way to attack a city! But Joshua trusted God. So he gave the orders to the Israelites.

Every day for six days they marched round Jericho. The armed guard led the way. Then came seven priests, blowing trumpets made from rams' horns. Next came the Ark of the Covenant, carried by more priests. Then came all the people. The only sounds were the blowing of the trumpets and the tramp, tramp, tramp of feet. The people inside the city waited in terror.

On the seventh day the Israelites started their march at dawn. This time they went round seven times. The seventh time, as the people completely surrounded the walls, the priests blew loudly on their trumpets. And Joshua cried, "Shout! The Lord God has given the city to you!"

Then the people yelled their war-cry – and the great walls of Jericho fell down flat!

Shouting in triumph, the Israelites swarmed into the city.

And they *knew* that God was with Joshua, their leader.

SAMSON AND DELILAH

Samson was chosen by God to help free the Israelites from their enemies, the Philistines. For years the Philistines tried to capture Samson. But God had given him great strength, and he always got away.

Then the Philistines discovered he was in love with a lady called Delilah. Slyly, they gave her money so that she would help them to trick him.

Pretending to tease, Delilah kept asking Samson how he could possibly be captured. Finally he told her. His strength was in his long hair. Delilah told the Philistines. And while he slept with his head in her lap, a man crept in and shaved Samson's head.

Now Samson was easily taken. Cruelly, the Philistines blinded him. They put chains on him. They made him do heavy work in a grinding mill. Samson was very unhappy. But God had not forgotten him. And his hair began to grow...

The Philistines held a celebration. They called for Samson to be brought, so that they could jeer at him. But with a mighty effort Samson pushed apart two pillars of the temple. The building crashed to the ground, killing everyone in it. And so Samson died, amongst his enemies.

RUTH AND NAOMI

◆

Naomi's husband and sons had died in Moab. Broken-hearted, Naomi wanted to return to her own land. Sadly she told her two daughters-in-law not to come with her. But one of them, Ruth, would not let Naomi be alone. "Nothing but death shall separate us!" Ruth promised. And the two of them journeyed on together.

SAMUEL

◆

Samuel's mother had pleaded with God, "If only You'll let me have a baby boy, I'll give him back to You. He shall serve You all his life."

Samuel was born; and she kept her promise. As soon as the boy was old enough, she brought him to live in the temple. There he learned to help Eli, the priest.

One night, Samuel was lying on his bed when he heard a voice. "Samuel!"

Quickly Samuel got up and ran to Eli. "Here I am!" he panted. "You called me."

Eli was puzzled. "I didn't call you! Go back to bed."

Samuel lay down. But again he heard the voice. "Samuel!"

He scrambled up, and ran to Eli. "Here I am. You *did* call me!"

"No!" Eli answered. "I didn't call you! Go and lie down!"

But once more the same thing happened. Then Eli realized that God Himself was calling Samuel.

"Go and lie down," Eli said. "If you hear the voice again, say 'Speak, Lord. Your servant is listening.'"

Once more Samuel lay down. Once more he heard, "Samuel!"

"Speak, Lord. Your servant is listening," said Samuel.

Then God gave him a very sad message. But when he told it to Eli, Eli said quietly, "Let God do whatever seems right to Him. He knows best."

As Samuel grew older everyone knew that God was with him; and they listened to his words.

DAVID AND GOLIATH

David the shepherd boy had come to bring food to his brothers who were in King Saul's army. Just as David reached them he heard a voice shouting across the valley, "If anyone defeats me single-handed, we will be your slaves. But if I defeat *him*, you shall be *our* slaves!"

It was the Philistine giant, Goliath!

David expected an Israelite to step forward to fight. Instead, they all ran to hide in their tents! David couldn't believe it! "I will fight this giant who dares to challenge the army of God's people!" he cried.

"You!" jeered his brothers. "You're just showing off!"

But King Saul sent for David. David said, "To protect my sheep I killed a lion and a bear. God saved me from harm then. He will save me now."

Then King Saul put his own armour on David; but it was so heavy, David couldn't

move! He took it off. With only his shepherd's rod and sling, David faced Goliath.

"You! A *boy*! I'll cut you in pieces and feed you to the birds!" roared the giant.

"God is with me!" David answered. "I will kill you! Then everyone will know He is the one true God!"

Furious, Goliath rushed forward. David put a pebble into his sling. He whirled the sling around, let go of one end – and out flew the pebble! It hit Goliath right in the middle of his forehead. And the giant fell down dead.

THE QUEEN OF SHEBA

The Queen of Sheba refused to believe the stories people were telling about the wisdom of Solomon.

"But they are true!" her servants cried.

"I shall go and see for myself!" declared the queen.

She set out across the desert, taking with her a great number of servants and many rich gifts.

King Solomon, splendidly dressed, awaited her. They greeted each other. Then the Queen of Sheba asked Solomon many difficult questions. But he answered each one wisely. She couldn't find anything he didn't know.

Presently Solomon took her to the entrance of the magnificent temple. She gazed at it. Then she cried, "It is enough! Everything people say about you *is* true! Blessed be the Lord your God, who has given you so much wisdom!"

She gave Solomon many gifts; and he gave her anything she asked for. Then the Queen of Sheba returned across the desert to her home; but it had been a splendid visit.

ELIJAH

Most of the Israelites in Ahab's kingdom had started to worship false gods. But Elijah still worshipped the true God.

God gave him a message for Ahab. Unless Elijah said so, there would be no rain or dew in the country – for years!

Elijah delivered the message; then rushed to hide from Ahab's anger in Kerith Ravine, as God instructed. And for as long as Elijah was there, God sent ravens carrying bread and meat in their beaks. They would drop the food and so Elijah was fed.

NAAMAN VISITS ELISHA

◆

Naaman, commander of the King of Aram's mighty army, had caught leprosy. He was in despair. But his wife owned a young Israelite slave girl. "If my master would go to our prophet Elisha, he could be healed!" the girl said.

Finally Naaman, with his chariots and horses, arrived at the door of Elisha's house. Elisha sent out a message. "Wash seven times in the River Jordan, and you will be healed."

"He doesn't speak to me himself!" cried the furious Naaman. "And our own rivers are surely better than the Jordan!"

At last his servants persuaded Naaman to try; and he was cured. Humbly, Naaman said to Elisha, "Your God is the true God; and I will worship Him."

ESTHER

◆

King Xerxes was drunk with wine. He sent for his wife Vashti, so that he could show off her beauty at his banquet. Vashti refused to come. King Xerxes' advisers told him he must banish her for ever, and find a new, beautiful young queen.

Esther was chosen. She was a Jew, but no one at court knew this, for Mordecai, who had brought her up, told her to keep it a secret. But later, Haman, a man who had found favour with the king, intended to kill all Jews because Mordecai would not bow down to him. Mordecai, deeply distressed, managed to get a message to Esther.

Bravely Esther told the king she, too, was a Jew. She pleaded with the king. The Jews were spared, and Haman was hung on the gallows he'd intended for Mordecai.

ISAIAH

Isaiah was a great prophet, and an adviser to four kings of Judah – Uzziah, Jothan, Ahaz and Hezekiah.

In the year that King Uzziah died Isaiah was in the temple when he saw a vision of God in all His glory. Seraphs with six wings were around God's throne. The seraphs called to one another, "Holy, Holy, Holy is the Lord Almighty!" Isaiah was afraid; but one of the seraphs flew to him, and told him his sins had been forgiven.

Then Isaiah was given a message from God to tell to the people. During his lifetime he was given many such messages. He always spoke them faithfully, although many of them were bad tidings.

He married a prophetess. They had two sons, one named Maher-Shalal-Hash-Baz (as God told Isaiah) and one named Shear-Jashub. The names had special meanings, reminding the people of what God intended to do.

The book which Isaiah wrote, and is part of the Bible, contains many of his prophecies, or messages. It looked forward to the time when a special child would be born – a child whom people would talk about as Wonderful Counsellor; Mighty God; Everlasting Father; and Prince of Peace.

DANIEL

King Darius had chosen Daniel to be chief ruler in Babylon. The other rulers were very jealous. "We'll get rid of him!" they plotted.

They knew Daniel worshipped the God of Israel. So they suggested to the king, "Make a law saying that for thirty days people can pray only to you. Anyone who disobeys will be thrown to the lions."

Darius nodded, pleased.

"The law must be written down!" said the rulers; for once their laws were written, they could never be changed.

Again Darius agreed. Gleefully the rulers watched him write.

Daniel realized at once the law was meant to trap him. He *could* save himself by not praying to God for thirty days... He could pray in secret... No. He went upstairs to the front room, stood by the windows which faced towards Jerusalem, and prayed to God to help him.

The rulers rushed to tell the king. Then *Darius* saw the trap. Deeply distressed, he watched as Daniel was thrown into the lions' den. "May the God to whom you are so faithful save you!" he cried.

He sealed the entrance, and returned to the palace. All night he lay awake. At dawn he rose, and hurried to the den. Fearfully he called, "Daniel! H*as* your God saved you?"

And Daniel answered, "Yes!"

Then Daniel was pulled out of the den. The rulers were thrown in. The lions killed them instantly. And Darius commanded that all his people should respect Daniel's great God.

JONAH

God spoke to Jonah. "Go to Nineveh. Tell the people they are so wicked their city is to be destroyed."

Jonah was afraid. The people might kill him for saying such a thing! He wouldn't go... He would hide from God!

Hastily, he caught a ship sailing for Tarshish, in the opposite direction from Nineveh. Down below decks he fell asleep, sure God could no longer see him.

Suddenly a great storm arose. The crew, terrified of sinking, prayed to their gods. They threw cargo overboard to lighten the ship. It was no use. The captain woke Jonah. "Pray to *your* God! Maybe H*e* will save us!"

"I worship the God who *made* the sea, yet I was trying to run away from Him," said Jonah. "You must throw me overboard."

First, the sailors tried to row for shore. It was impossible. So they threw Jonah over the side. And the storm died away.

Down sank Jonah, afraid he would drown. But God sent a great fish which swallowed him whole. Three days later, at God's command, the fish coughed Jonah up on to a beach.

Jonah lay there, gasping. And God spoke again. "Go to Nineveh!"

This time, Jonah went. Trembling, he gave the people God's message. To his amazement, they believed him. The king commanded everyone to pray for forgiveness; and to show they were truly sorry, they must wear sackcloth and neither eat nor drink.

When God saw this, He forgave the people. Nineveh was saved.

19

THE NEW TESTAMENT

ELIZABETH AND ZACHARIAS

One day, as Zacharias the priest worked in the temple, the angel Gabriel appeared to him. "Your wife Elizabeth is to have the son you prayed for," said Gabriel. "You must call him John. He is to be very special. He will tell the people to be ready for the Messiah – the Saviour."

"But my wife and I are too old to have a baby!" protested Zacharias.

Gabriel spoke sternly. "Since you do not believe God's message, you shall be dumb until the day it happens!"

In time Elizabeth *did* have a baby boy. Her family and friends were glad for her. And they were sure the baby would be named Zacharias, after his father.

"No!" said Elizabeth. "He is to be called John."

"But no one in your family is called John!" they cried. They turned to Zacharias, sure *he* would agree with them.

Zacharias made signs asking for a writing tablet. To their amazement, he wrote, "His name is John." At once Zacharias was able to speak again. He began praising God.

Then everyone wondered about this special child…

He grew up to be John the Baptist. He lived in the desert. And he *did* tell people to be ready for the coming of the Messiah – his cousin, Jesus.

SIMEON AND ANNA

Simeon lived in Jerusalem. He was an old man, but God had promised he would not die until he had seen the Messiah.

Simeon waited, and prayed. And one day God said to him, "Go to the temple *today*. Today you will find the Messiah there."

Trembling with excitement, Simeon made his way to the temple as fast as he could. It was crowded with people. Which one was the Messiah?

Then Mary and Joseph came into the temple courts, carrying Baby Jesus. And Simeon *knew*. Shakily, he said to Mary, "Please may I hold Him?" His face was full of love. Mary put Jesus into his arms.

Then Mary and Joseph listened in amazement, for Simeon began to praise God.

"You have kept Your promise, Lord! Now I can die in peace. The light which shines here shall shine for all nations."

After he had spoken some more words, Simeon gently handed Jesus back to Mary.

Anna, a very old lady who was always in the temple, came up to them.

"This is the Messiah!" she cried. She thanked God, and told everyone there, "This is the Saviour!"

Mary and Joseph carried out the ceremony of presenting the Baby Jesus to God, which was the law. They made a thanks-offering of two turtle doves. Then they took the tiny baby back to Bethlehem, to rest for a while.

But Mary never forgot those extraordinary happenings in the temple.

JESUS' DISCIPLES

Jesus had grown up now. He started on His work of telling people about God's Kingdom; and He chose twelve men to be His disciples – His special helpers.

There were four fishermen – Simon (later called Peter); Andrew, Peter's brother; James, son of Zebedee; and John, his brother, who was known as 'the beloved disciple'.

There was also Philip; Thaddeus; James, son of Alphaeus; Nathaniel, sometimes called Bartholomew; Simon the Zealot; Matthew, a tax-collector (who later wrote one of the Gospels); Judas Iscariot, who was to betray Jesus to His enemies; and Thomas, also called Didymus, or 'twin'.

JAIRUS' DAUGHTER

One day, Jairus, a ruler of the Synagogue, came to Jesus. "My twelve-year-old daughter is dying! Please come!" he begged.

Jesus set out with him; but He paused to heal a woman. As they moved on again, men from Jairus' house came running. "Don't trouble the Master," they cried. "Your daughter is dead!"

Jesus spoke gently. "Trust Me, Jairus! She will be healed."

Outside the house people were wailing and crying. "Hush!" said Jesus. "She's not dead – only asleep." They laughed at Him. Did He think they didn't know the difference?

Jesus sent everyone out of the room except three of His disciples, the girl's mother, and Jairus. Quietly, He took the girl's hand. "Child – wake up!" He said.

And the girl who had been dead sat up, and was perfectly well!

THE BOY WITH THE LOAVES AND FISHES

All day the boy had been one of the crowd of people on the hillside listening to Jesus. Now he heard Jesus' disciples say to Him, "Tell the people to go and find food before it gets too dark!"

"*You* feed them!" said Jesus.

"It would cost eight months' wages!" cried Philip.

"Find out how much food we have already," answered Jesus.

Shyly, the boy went up to Andrew, one of the disciples. Andrew took him to Jesus, saying, "There is a boy here with five barley loaves and two small fishes... But what use are they amongst so many?"

"Tell the people to sit down," said Jesus. He took the loaves and fishes, blessed them, and gave them to the disciples to share out. The boy was amazed! There was enough for everyone – with twelve baskets of scraps left over! Through his gift to Jesus, five thousand people had been fed.

THE TEN LEPERS

Ten lepers waited anxiously. Jesus was going to pass by...

At last they saw Him coming. "Master!" they shouted. "Please help us!"

Jesus called back, "Go and show yourselves to the priest!"

Hoping against hope, the lepers obeyed. And as they went, their leprosy cleared. They were cured! One of them, a Samaritan, ran back. "Thank you, Jesus!" he cried.

Jesus said, "Weren't there ten of you? Where are the other nine? Go on your way. Your faith has healed you."

BARTIMAEUS

◆

Bartimaeus lived in Jericho. He was blind. There was no work he could do, so all through the hot, dusty days he had to sit at the roadside begging for money. Otherwise he would have starved.

One day as he sat there he heard the sound of many excited voices in the distance. "What's happening?" he cried.

Someone nearby answered, "Jesus of Nazareth is going to come this way!"

Jesus – who had made blind people see! If only Bartimaeus could get to Him! ...But how could he possibly find Jesus in a crowd, without being able to *see*?

He decided what he would do. He waited; waited until he could tell the crowd was passing right in front of him. Then he shouted loudly, "Jesus! Jesus of Nazareth!"

"Be quiet!" said some of the people.

But Bartimaeus would not be quiet. "Jesus!" he shouted desperately. "Help me!"

Jesus heard. Quietly he said, "Bring that man to Me."

Hands urged Bartimaeus to his feet. "Come to Jesus!" said someone.

Trembling, Bartimaeus went with them. He heard Jesus' voice ask gently, "What do you want Me to do?"

"If only I could have my sight!" cried Bartimaeus.

"Your faith has healed you," said Jesus. And immediately, Bartimaeus could see! Joyfully he gave thanks to God. And all the crowd praised God, and were glad with him.

ZACCHAEUS

Zacchaeus was a tax-collector. He had become rich by cheating people. Nobody liked him, and he was very lonely.

One day he heard people calling, "Jesus is coming!"

Zacchaeus wanted to see Jesus! He hurried outside. But there were crowds of people lining the street – and he was a very short man. He tried to squeeze to the front; but when they saw who he was no one would let him through.

Zacchaeus was desperate. Then he had an idea. Further down the road was a sycamore tree... Zacchaeus raced along behind the backs of the people. Breathless, hot, he climbed the tree... *Now* he could see!

Jesus was coming, getting closer and closer... He stopped. He looked straight up into the tree. "Zacchaeus!" He said. "Come down! Today I must stay at your house!"

Jesus had noticed him! And wanted to *stay* with him! Zacchaeus could hardly believe it. Joyfully he scrambled down.

Now *he* was walking along the road with Jesus. The crowd muttered angrily, "Jesus is going to visit the house of that cheat!"

Zacchaeus heard them. "Master," he said, "I'll give half my belongings to the poor. And if I've cheated anyone, I'll pay him back four times as much!"

The listening people gasped. But Jesus said to them, "Remember, the Son of Man has come specially to people who have done wrong, so that they can be sorry, and God can forgive them."

And He and Zacchaeus walked on together.

MARY, MARTHA AND LAZARUS ◆

Mary and Martha were sisters, friends of Jesus. Their brother Lazarus was very sick, so they sent for Jesus. But Jesus delayed His coming; and Lazarus died.

When at last Jesus was near, Martha ran to meet Him. "If You had been here, Lazarus wouldn't have died!" she cried.

Jesus answered quietly, "Whoever lives and believes in Me shall never die. Do you believe this?"

Martha looked into His face. "I do," she said. She hastened to tell Mary that Jesus had come. Mary ran to Him, greeting Him as Martha had done.

Seeing their sorrow, Jesus wept. Then He went to the tomb; and after praying to God called, "Lazarus! Come out!"

And Lazarus came out of the tomb – alive again.

THE WIDOW IN THE TEMPLE ◆

It was getting close to the time when Jesus knew He must be crucified. As He sat in the temple one day He noticed a poor lady whose husband had died. She crept up to the offering box and dropped in two small coins, ashamed that her offering was so small.

But Jesus said, "I tell you, this lady has given more than all the rich people who drop silver and gold into the box! Because she loves God, she has given Him all the money she had. No one can ever give more than that."

The widow felt very happy; but the people in authority were angry at His teaching.

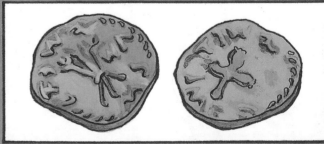

PETER

Jesus had been crucified; but He had risen to life again! The disciples had seen Him!

Now seven of them – including Peter – waited by the shores of Lake Tiberias, longing to see Him again. Peter was especially upset. Before Jesus was crucified he had said three times he didn't even know Him...

Suddenly Peter cried, "I'm going fishing!" The others went with him. They fished all night, but caught nothing. At dawn they rowed sadly towards the shore.

There was someone on the beach... He called to them, "Cast your net on the other side of the boat!" Wondering, they obeyed.

The net came up full of fish – and John cried, "It is the Lord!"

Peter sprang out of the boat and splashed ashore. There was a fire there, with fish cooking on it. As the others landed, Jesus said, "Bring over some of *your* fish."

Peter rushed across, and pulled the loaded net in all by himself.

They ate breakfast together, there on the shore. Then, three times – as many times as Peter had said he didn't know Jesus – Jesus asked, "Simon Peter – do you love Me?"

Each time Peter answered in distress, "Lord, You *know* I love You!" The last time he added, "You know *everything*!"

And Jesus said, "Care for My followers, and My little ones."

Peter was comforted. Jesus had forgiven him; and had trusted him with special work for God's Kingdom.

THE LAME MAN

In Jerusalem there lived a man who couldn't walk. Every day he sat by the gate called Beautiful and begged for money to buy food.

One afternoon he saw Peter and John coming. He called to them, "Please! Give me whatever you can spare!"

Jesus had gone back to Heaven now, but the disciples were still carrying on His work. Peter said, "I have no silver and gold, but what I *do* have I give to you! In the name of Jesus Christ of Nazareth – get up and walk!"

And to the amazement of the watching people, the lame man tried to stand – and found he was healed!

PHILIP AND THE ETHIOPIAN

Philip, one of Jesus' disciples, was puzzled. God had told him to go to a lonely stretch of desert road. But why?

Presently he saw a chariot approaching. The Holy Spirit said to him, "Go across to that chariot. Stay with it."

Still puzzled, Philip obeyed. As he ran along, he saw that in the chariot was an Ethiopian, trying to understand some words written by Isaiah. *Now* Philip knew why he had been sent there!

"I can help you!" he cried.

Gladly the Ethiopian listened as Philip explained that Isaiah had been talking about Jesus. Philip told the whole story of Jesus; and the Ethiopian believed. "Can I be baptized as Jesus was?" he asked. "Now? In that water by the roadside?"

So Philip baptized him; and the Ethiopian continued on his way, full of joy.

PAUL

After the crucifixion, Saul had been one of the keenest people to search out the followers of Jesus. He wanted them to be killed because he thought their beliefs were wrong.

But from the beginning Jesus had chosen Saul to be His messenger, both to the Jews and to the people of other races. So, in a blinding light, He Himself spoke to Saul on the Damascus road. And Saul, too, became a believer.

His preaching was so powerful that the Jewish rulers in Damascus decided *he* must be killed. "We'll watch the city gates, and catch him as he goes through!" they said.

Saul's friends warned him of the plot. "You must escape over the wall!" they cried. But the walls were strong and high...

At last they had an idea. They fastened ropes to a large basket. That night Saul climbed into the basket – and his friends lowered him down through an opening in the wall!

He got safely away. From then on he had many adventures as he journeyed round telling people the good news of Jesus, and explaining how God wanted them to live.

He made many enemies, who thought his beliefs were wrong. He was beaten and imprisoned; but nothing could stop him from carrying out his task for God.

He became known as Paul. While he was in prison he wrote many letters – wise letters, full of hope. And we can still read some of them today, in the Bible.

INDEX

A Abraham 7; Ahab 15; Ahaz 17; Alphaeus 22; Andrew 22, 23; Anna 21; Asher 3

B Bartimaeus 24; Benjamin 3

D Dan 3; Daniel 18; Darius 18; David 14; Delilah 12; Didymus (Thomas) 22

E Eli 13; Elijah 15; Elisha 16; Elizabeth 20; Esau 8; Esther 16

G Gabriel 20; Gad 3; Goliath 14

H Haman 16; Hezekiah 17

I Isaac 7, 8; Isaiah 17, 28; Issachar 2

J Jacob 2, 8; Jairus 22; James, son of Alphaeus 22; James, son of Zebedee 22; Jesus 20-29; Jochabed 10; John, the disciple 22, 31; John the Baptist 20; Jonah 19; Joseph 3, 9, 21; Joshua 11; Jothan 17; Judah 2; Judas Iscariot 22

K King of Aram 16

L Laban 8; Lazarus 26; Levi 2; Lot's wife 7; Luke 31

M Maher-Shalal-Hash-Baz 17; Mark 31; Martha 26; Mary 21; Mary, sister of Lazarus 26; Matthew 22, 31; Miriam 10; Mordecai 16; Moses 10

N Naaman 16; Naomi 13; Naphtali 3; Nathaniel 22; Noah 6

P Peter 22, 27, 28; Philip 22, 23, 28

Q Queen of Sheba 15

R Reuben 2, 9; Ruth 13

S Samson 12; Samuel 13; Saul, King 14; Saul, later called Paul 29; Shear-Jashub 17; Simeon 2, 21; Simon, later called Peter 22, 27; Simon the Zealot 22

T Thaddeus 22; Thomas (Didymus) 22

U Uzziah 17

V Vashti 16

X Xerxes 16

Z Zacchaeus 25; Zacharias 20; Zebedee 22; Zebulun 2